THE BOY, THE CAT

AND

THE BOX IN THE ATTIC

BY
SHEILA WHYMAN

For Stuart, Scott, Steph and Chrissie

Chapter One

Jamie versus Bad Billy

Jamie looked in the mirror, forgetting for a moment, the toothbrush in his hand and the teeth cleaning he was supposed to be engaged in.

"Yipee! Today's the last day of school," he shouted with pure joy in his voice, as spots of toothpaste splashed against the glass.

He danced around the bathroom like he was performing a war dance. He smiled and winked at his reflection, gave a bloodcurdling whoop and smiled again. School was not his favourite place, not like it used to be.

Finally, the end of the summer term was here and Jamie was looking forward to the days of freedom he would spend with Gran in her ancient, but interesting house in the country. The night before, he and his mum had packed his case and he was all set to go. Just a short day at school then he would start his great adventure. One day, that was all!

"Jamie, have you finished in the bathroom yet?" Mum was calling him from the kitchen..... For how long? Jamie didn't know. She sounded cross. "You'll be late for school," she bellowed.

Jamie hurried downstairs. He knew he was too late for breakfast, so he grabbed an apple from the fruit bowl , wrenched open the door and ran out. As he banged the door shut, he shouted goodbye in the direction of the kitchen, hoping mum had calmed down but he could still hear her grumbling, as he went down the path. Oh well. She'd get over it! He smiled again.

On the way to school, he met up with 'Bad Billy Braithwaite' and his gang. What a motley crew! No-one called him 'Bad Billy' to his face, of course, but bad he was and bad he always would be. Billy and his gang hated Jamie or so it seemed, because they picked on him whenever they could. Today was no different, for there was Billy, with the gleam in his eye, which Jamie knew meant trouble. His smile disappeared.

"Eh, lads, what've we got here, then? An apple for the teacher, eh Jellyboy."

Jamie hated that name. It referred to the time when he had refused to eat anything but jelly and ice-cream. A time when he was ridiculed by those around him. The fad was short-lived, but the name had stuck, particularly in Billy's mind. He cringed and waited.

"What a surprise if teacher got it from me, eh Jellyboy! Give it here and let's see what she says."

Billy made a grab for the apple. Jamie knew it was useless trying to stop the bully so he meekly handed the apple over.

"It seems I haven't any choice, Billy." Jamie said, adding in a whisper "But one of these days 'Bad Bill Braithwaite', you'll regret it. I promise you that!"

"What was that, Jellyboy? Did I hear a threat? P'raps a sharp clip round the earhole will help you forget this little...erm...mistake? See to it Mouse. "Billy ordered.

Mouse was a rather obnoxious, giant of a boy, who liked nothing better than to torment smaller boys. He had a very mean streak. He set about Jamie with great gusto, catching his ear with one almighty blow from his huge fist. It sent Jamie reeling, to eventually sprawl face down on the floor at Billy's feet.

"Shall I give him a kick for good luck, Billy? Just to do it right" sneered Mouse.

"Na," laughed Billy. "Why waste time on him. I can see our friend Tommyboy coming down the road. He's always good for some fun AND money at the end of it. Come on, leave Jellyboy there. Bye Jel. Thanks for the loan of this."

With a toss of the apple, 'Bad Billy' raised his hand and waved goodbye. After he had disappeared around the corner, well out of earshot, Jamie repeated his warning.

"One of these days, Billy Braithwaite. You wait and see. I'm gonna get you!"

It was all wishful thinking of course. He hadn't the faintest idea what he would do to get even, but he would think of something. Very soon!

Once at school, Jamie forgot the apple, even though it stood mocking him from the teacher's desk. Mrs Wright had been very surprised and very suspicious when Billy had presented it to her. As he handed it over, he gave the rest of the class a wicked grin. Looking at Billy's face, Jamie remembered the fist and the threat of a kicking. He would not forget. He would store up those bad times and remember them later.   Still there were better things to think about now. Soon he would be on his way to Gran's ancient and mysterious house.

Chapter Two

Jamie and Billy

All that last day at school Jamie could not concentrate, even though their teacher had devised fun activities for them to try. His mind drifted between his adventures to come at Gran's house and the incident with Billy on his way to school; Two very different trains of thought, one full of joy and excitement, the other full of fear and regret.

Fun games at school reminded him that Bad Billy had not always been the enemy, the bully that everyone in his class feared. He was once a rather shy, timid little boy with whom Jamie had begun his school career. They had rolled up together on their first day at nursery, two little kids both wanting yet hating to leave their mums at the gate.

Jamie had been the first to let go of his mum's hand and venture a few steps towards a tall woman, smiling a welcome to all her 'little ones'. Billy had hesitated, turning his head away from the kindly woman a large tear rolling down his cheek and falling silently to the floor. .

"Come on everyone. I've got some fun games inside that we can all play with," she called in a sweet sing-song voice.

This made Billy hold on to his mother's hand even more tightly, his tears falling faster while his mouth emitted small whimpering sounds. On hearing those sounds, Jamie turned back and marched confidently towards Billy.

"Come on Bill. It'll be ok. Our mums will be back soon and there's fun games inside." He took Billy's other hand and gently led him towards the building.

Jamie was not as confident as he sounded but figured that they could face this big adventure together. And so it was for the next four years.

Gradually, however things began to change, which forged a wedge between the two boys and destroyed their friendship. As time went by Jamie, always ready to try new ideas and activities , began to outshine Billy both in school and out, He always came top of the class in everything he tried and was popular, making friends easily with his kind, easy-going manner. Both children and adults liked Jamie.

Billy, on the other hand, found schoolwork hard and the more he tried, the more he got confused and upset, becoming sullen and uncommunicative. Jamie tried to help, showing Billy the way in his usual gentle manner but as the years progressed Billy began to develop a resentment towards his best friend.

"You think you're SO clever, Jamie, don't you? Proper teacher's pet," he would whisper scathingly as Jamie answered yet another question to which Billy had no idea of the answer. Maths, English, History, Science – there was nothing at which Jamie didn't do well.

Billy's whispered comments became louder as the years went by and he took every opportunity to push Jamie 'accidently' or try to make him look a fool. He began to treat others in the same way and took great delight in their pain. His teachers could not help but notice and his mum was called into school on several occasions to discuss his behaviour. Exasperated, Mum then told him, how disappointed she was in him and that things must change. But they never did. His yearly reports pointed out his failings, both learning and behavioural, in a never-ending monotony. His parents dreaded the end of the school year as they began to realise that his reports were getting worse. Arguments marked their arrival and in final desperation they would shout.

"Why can't you be more like Jamie Tyler!"

The final blow came when both Billy and Jamie tried out for the local under tens football team. Billy was more excited than he'd been for a while, believing that he was much better at football than anyone else in his class. In school games, he always had the ball and always scored the goals. Jamie got nowhere near the ball. What he didn't know was that the boys secretly played football when he wasn't around and Jamie was a very good player.

At the start of the trial, everything went well for Billy. The boys gave him the ball without trying for it themselves. Little did he know that they were too scared to do otherwise. Then Billy was called off the pitch and replaced by Jamie. The game changed and they began to play as a team.

At the end of the trial, the coach called all the excited boys together for the final team list. Ten names were read out, none of them Billy or Jamie's. Excitement grew as other boys found out that they were in the team.

"And finally," the coach paused to check his notes, "The team striker, because he showed both skill and teamwork is.... Jamie Tyler. Congratulations, lad."

Billy's face contorted in rage.

Jamie's thoughts returned to the present. The apple still mocked him from the teacher's desk. He looked at it. Billy was once his best friend but now he hated him...

Chapter Three

Jamie Starts His Adventure

"Gran will be at the other end to meet you, Jamie. Now don't forget to watch for the right station."

He was not listening. He was planning the things he was going to do over the next six weeks.

"Are you listening to me, Jamie? Mum's voice was high-pitched with agitation, getting louder as she went on. "You'll get lost, you know... if you don't watch out. Then where will you be. Lost in some strange...."

"Muuum! Shhhh! People are looking." Jamie whispered. "Don't worry. I'll be OK. I've been before. Stop fussing. I know where I'm going," he added.

Actually, Jamie was very sure where he was going... on an adventure... and he wasn't going to miss any part of it, let alone get lost. With a smile to reassure his mum, he got on the train. It pulled out of the station almost immediately. The final sight he saw, through the carriage window, was mum, hand in the air, looking cross, but sad. Oh well. She'll get over it. She and dad were going to the Caribbean! Jamie smiled.

The journey was short and uneventful. Jamie read his fishing magazine and planned the weeks ahead. He was going to spend every day at the riverside, fishing! He clutched his fishing rods tightly, he didn't care if he lost his case and his clothes, as long as he didn't lose those. He grinned. Even his best friend, Luke, had laughed at him preferring to catch fish than to go on a great holiday abroad. And yet, that was exactly what he was going to do: Go fishing instead of flying to the Caribbean with his mum and dad. Luke had been struck dumb with amazement when Jamie first told him. Recovering quickly, he had asked if he could go instead then he had laughed out loud. Jamie was hurt. Not one of his friends liked fishing. More fool them...

Gran said he took after Granddad who had loved fishing too. When Jamie was quite small, Granddad had taught Jamie to fish. He missed his grandfather, and the days at the river, fishing and laughing and mucking about. Thoughts of Granddad made him feel sad. Gran must really miss him. Perhaps he would spend a few days at home with her, or maybe invite her to come fishing too. He grinned again. He was not sure: - Did Gran like fishing?

She was there, of course, at the station, just as she had promised, a bright, cheery face in a sea of other faces, less bright and cheery. He saw her straight away, waving a psychedelic scarf in his direction. Gran was a bit weird, she liked fast cars, motor bikes and a fairground rides. Not necessarily in that order! She dressed in bright clothes which never seemed to match. Today she was wearing a purple floor-length coat, the open front revealing a long, fluorescent - orange dress with blue and yellow swirls on it. Mum said she was a one off, a throwback to the seventies, whatever that meant! Jamie thought Gran was great. Mum thought Gran was mad. Everyone else just didn't know what to think. At that moment, Gran saw him and waved again, jumping up and down so her skirt jiggled about and nearly tripped her up. Jamie laughed, looked at her and thought he was really going to enjoy this holiday. Gran was fun and the river and fishing waited. He walked quickly towards her.

So you got here then?" Gran said in a voice which was much too loud. "Let's go. I've got the car parked on double yellow lines and some Cola waiting at home."

"No motor bike then, Gran?" he asked.

"Now what would your mum say to that?" Gran replied.

Jamie didn't like to think. He'd heard Mum talking to Dad on that subject, where words like, crazy... lunatic and dangerous were mentioned. It was worth asking though just in case Gran gave in one day. He desperately wanted a ride on her motor bike. Maybe one day? Brisk, as usual, the journey to Gran's house was made with the minimum of fuss and the maximum speed. Gran really was an excellent driver although that's not what Mum would have said!

Jamie was very tired after his journey. More tired than he wanted to admit. He drank the cola, told Gran they could catch up on all the news in the morning and went gratefully to a very comfortable bed.

It took a while for him to re- adjust to Gran's bizarre house decoration but soon he was snuggled down under his multi-coloured duvet, in his multi-coloured room, thinking of the good times ahead. The adventure had begun. If you could call six weeks of non-stop fishing an adventure which Luke certainly wouldn't but Jamie certainly would. Little did Jamie know, in bed on that first night, the real adventure had yet to begin. But soon, so very soon it would, and there would be no turning away from it once it had started.

Chapter Four

Jamie Finds the Book

It would have to rain. Jamie was livid. Only two days of fishing and it had started to pour, never to stop. He had read his magazine a zillion times and he was BORED! He did not like to admit it but he now wished he had gone to the Caribbean with his mum and dad. Even a bumpy plane ride and travel sickness was better than boredom. It surely could not be worse than this nightmare. Gran had tried very hard to cheer him up. She had suggested trips into town, bowling and the cinema but Jamie hated every one of her ideas. To be honest, he was just so annoyed that the weather could do this to him. How unkind of it, to rain and spoil HIS long thought-out and anticipated plans. It was SO unfair.

Like all people who are bored and annoyed, he was not pleasant to be with. He banged about the house, sighed and tut-tutted at every little thing. And he was extremely rude and unkind to Gran, who, after all was only trying to do her best.

"For goodness sake, Jamie," shouted Gran. He could tell she was angry, because she was pounding the pastry she was making, into the table and it was making a terrible noise. " Find something useful to do. Go and read your magazine, look at a book, go to sleep! Anything. But get out of my hair for an hour or two." Gran ordered in an exasperated voice.

This was so unlike Gran that Jamie scooted out of the kitchen double fast, narrowly missing Gran's treasured 'Egyptian' sphinx. He ran upstairs ready to call Gran all the names he could think of and have a good sulk. It was then that he suddenly stopped and spotted the door. It was at the top of another flight of stairs just waiting for him. Had he seen that door before? He must have, but he just didn't remember it. Now, because he was fed up, bored out of his brain, he was ready to try anything. Should he look behind the door? It beckoned. He did not hesitate. Up the extra flight of stairs he went, curiosity getting the better of him.

The door creaked ajar with a gentle touch. He pushed it harder, opening it further, seeing as he entered, a rather dark and dusty attic room, cluttered and neglected, cobwebs hanging from the rafters. Dark shapes promised boxes full of unknown treasures and he thought he spied granddad's old fishing rods in a corner. What a find! There must be lots of interesting and exciting stuff up here, thought Jamie. He could spend hours delving into boxes, sorting and playing with what he found. Perhaps the day was not going to be quite as bad as he thought. He found the switch and put on the light.

Two hours later saw Jamie knee-deep in old pictures, clothes and any number of odd things which he could not put a name to. He was just about to open a most interesting looking box, when he heard his grandmother's voice, calling from the kitchen.

"Jamie. Where are you? I didn't mean to be so cross earlier. Come down and have a drink and something to eat."

Jamie wanted to open the box.

"I'm OK Gran. I'll be down later. I've found something to do like you said. Don't worry."

Jamie wanted to open the box. He could not say why exactly, but he needed to open the box. Right now.

He did not know what he expected to find but it was most certainly not a box full of old tatty books. What a disappointment! They were beautiful; he had to admit, yet old and worn out. Nothing great here then. Maybe in his imagination, he thought he might find treasure in the box, an old pirate's treasure, or a map or something. It looked like a treasure box. The old wood was scarred and worn but it felt smooth to the touch as if many hands had felt its contours. He peered more closely inside and reaching in with his hand, lifted out the first book, turned it over and inspected it. It was ancient. He could see that, by the way it was much worn in several places. The cover was made from red leather, inlaid with what he suspected were pieces of gold. Perhaps he had found treasure after all.

When he gently turned over the book. , it opened at a place where it had obviously been opened many times before. The page was grubby where fingers had touched it countless times in the past.

Jamie began to read, finding it hard to contain his excitement. He gasped at what he read and read it again to make absolutely sure,

Chapter Five

The Real Adventure Begins

Jamie could not believe what he saw, it really was a spell book. He laughed at himself.

"Well, Jamie, you are, without doubt an out and out nutcase!" he muttered aloud. "A spell book. Who are you trying to fool. Nobody finds a spell book, except in those silly kid's stories."

It must be some kind of joke. Perhaps some boy long ago had been bored too and thought he'd have a good laugh at his expense . It had worked well; because Jamie half believed that the book and spells were real. What fun it would be though if the spells did work, especially this one. He read the description again. It seemed that with this spell, you could turn yourself or anyone else into a cat. Jamie had visions of prowling downstairs and scaring Gran half to death, as she met a black panther or a tiger or a magnificent lion. Serve her right. He still hadn't forgiven her. 'Just follow these instructions', it said. It was that simple. Yeah, right!

"Ha." This was highly amusing. A pity the person, who had thought of the joke, could not be there to see Jamie now, sitting goggle-eyed, thinking about trying the ridiculous spell, believing this stupid lie. He gave himself a mental shake. He was only thinking he might try it. How stupid!

"First put on the gold chain and pendant," he read aloud. He could not find it.

"That's it then," he uttered in disappointment. Then drawn by some mysterious urge, he looked again inside the box. There it was, winking wickedly at him from under the next book: The pendant. He pulled it out and stared at it, as if it would jump up and bite him. And it seemed as if it might have done exactly that. For on the cat shaped pendant were engraved five letters:

$$J - A - M - I - E$$

A cold shiver ran down Jamie's spine. This was a bit too much. This was taking the joke a little bit too far. It was just a coincidence that this pendant should have HIS name on it. That was enough now. It was somebody's idea of a sick joke and it wasn't very funny. No-one was laughing. His mind searched for someone who could have done this but it was impossible. No-one could have set this up, could they? His thoughts wandered towards Gran. She did have a weird sense of humour after all. And she knew Jamie wouldn't take it seriously, didn't she ? But he was. HE WAS! No he wasn't...Gran would be downstairs. giggling knowingly, expecting Jamie to run to her laughing at her joke.

Jamie smiled; the shock gone. He had sat there thinking for more than an hour. It might be fun to carry out the spell. It might work. He was almost sure it wouldn't. He was almost sure it was Grans little joke. Or maybe it wasn't Gran but some wizard ancestor who hid this just for him. And so his thoughts yo-yoed from one story to the other. Ah well. He had nothing better to do. He could still hear the rain, splashing relentlessly onto the roof above his head. He put on the pendant. It felt heavy around his neck. If nothing happened, he might ask Gran if he could keep it anyway, as a memento of an interesting afternoon.

Instruction two was to read five words aloud. Co-incidence, that it matched the number of letters on the pendant. He read them. They made no sense. This really WAS a joke. Nice one Gran. He would look back at this afternoon and think how crazy he had been yet somehow the urge to go on was too strong to resist. It was only a game after all.

"Magic..... Invades..... All.... Our..... Worlds....!"

The words were there in the book, and Jamie said them. He half expected a flash of light, as if this was happening in one of the comics he sometimes read. There was no light, not even a flicker. In fact, nothing happened at all.

He hadn't expected anything to happen anyway, he thought. Jamie was disappointed. Of course, he knew all along that nothing would happen. Nevertheless, you could always hope., couldn't you? It had been fun anyway: Imagining. Nice one Gran.

Jamie thinking of Gran, felt a zing of regret flash sharply through his mind. He had better go down and apologise for his rude behaviour. It had been a very long time since he had stormed out of the kitchen.

He got up and walked towards the door. Maybe he would come up here later because there was still more to investigate. It would waste a few more hours, until the sun came out again. At the door, Jamie turned to take one last look at the attic and caught sight of himself in a long-forgotten mirror.

NO!

He looked again. There staring back at him was not his face at all. It was a face he did not recognise. His green eyes shone out from the face of a sleek black cat. Not a panther. Not a tiger. Not even a magnificent lion but a small black cat. This cannot be true, he thought. But it was and Jamie at that moment did not know what he was going to do next.

Chapter Six

Jamie in Trouble

The problem was that Jamie did not know how to reverse the spell. He had tried to look at the book again but he could not seem to read it. It was blurred, as if he needed glasses. What was he going to do? He slowly went down the stairs and into his room to think. He lay down on the bed and tried very hard to come up with a solution.

He must have fallen asleep, because the next thing he knew was the sound of Gran's voice, shouting.

"Shoo! Go away. Get off Jamie's bed, you bad cat!"

Jamie was startled for a moment. Why was Gran still cross with him? Had she found out about his afternoon with her private things in the attic? Then he realised that she would not know that the black cat sleeping on the bed was indeed him. He scuttled away downstairs and out of the open back door. It had stopped raining, he noticed. No consolation, he couldn't go fishing like this. He simply had to find out how to turn back. It would have been funny if the thought of remaining a cat for the rest of his life was not uppermost in his mind. He was scared.

Jamie hid. Jamie hid, simply because he didn't know what else to do. The afternoon became evening and as night fell, he began to panic. He had not thought ahead, when he had tried that spell. He was so sure it wouldn't work; He was so sure it was Gran's joke. Now he was hungry and thirsty and miserable. Oh, how he wished he had read the whole page before saying those stupid words. The situation was made worse by the fact that Jamie knew that Gran was worried. She had called his name often, both inside and outside the house. How was she to know that her silly, adventurous grandson was outside, under a bush, hiding! Jamie crept nearer to the house. After many attempts, he managed to jump onto the kitchen window ledge and peer in. Inside he could see Gran with a frown on her face. She looked as if she had been crying.

What a stupid idiot, Jamie, how could he have done this to Gran, he thought? He was near to tears now. Could cats cry, he wondered? Gran, seeing the strange cat again, peeping in through the window, and having a soft heart, ambled to the back door and let in the sorry-looking creature. It looked as if too was crying. What a fanciful thought. The cat immediately rubbed itself around her legs. Jamie so wanted to tell her not to worry. That he would be back soon, but he knew that was impossible. Poor Gran. Poor Jamie.

Later that night, it was obvious to Jamie that Gran was worried. He lay curled on a chair and listened while she dialled 999. He wanted to tell her that he felt as miserable and frightened as she did. What a mess! The police arrived within twenty minutes. A pleasant looking young man in uniform came into the hall, when she answered the door. . On a different occasion Gran might have complained that policemen were getting younger and younger but not today. She simply began to explain:-

"It's so unlike Jamie to go off without saying anything. I know he was upset because I was cross with him, but I thought we'd....."

The policeman interrupted:-

"You said on the telephone that he often goes fishing at the river. Do you think he went there?"

Gran froze.

"Do you think he might have fallen in?" she asked, shock making her face pale. "No, it can't be that. He wouldn't have gone without telling me. Besides it has been raining for the best part of the day. Too wet to fish."

Jamie wanted to shout that he was still here, couldn't she see but it was a vain hope. He had to do something.

He left Gran talking quietly to the policeman and went up to his room to think some more. What was he going to do? How many times had he asked himself that question in the last few hours? He looked in the mirror. The same black cat looked back. He turned his back on the disturbing reflection and went back to the attic. There might be clues he had overlooked.

Nothing. No clues. Jamie was desperate. He turned quickly as he heard noises downstairs. The policeman was ready to leave. He can't go yet, thought Jamie, he hasn't found me.

" Look up here he begged I've been in the house all the time."

He heard the front door open, and as it shut, the strong wind that was blowing outside, caught in the hallway, blew up the stairs and banged the attic door shut. The noise crashed in Jamie's ears as he looked unbelievingly at the door. Trapped!

"Think like a cat," he told himself. "What would a cat do, if it were locked in somewhere?" He would cry for help!

Jamie, after a few croaky tries, began to meow loudly. Soon he heard Gran coming up the stairs. Had she heard him? Suddenly the attic door creaked open. Gran stood silhouetted in the doorway. Jamie tried to push past her. He wanted to rush downstairs away from the worried look he had seen on Gran's face. Gran looked long and hard at him.

"And what do you think you're doing up here, young man? You've worried your poor Gran so much I don't know whether I'm coming or going. I've looked everywhere for you, you naughty boy!"

-The words were angry, but Gran looked and sounded relieved as she hugged Jamie tightly. Jamie knew how she felt. He was relieved too. He had found, quite by accident, how to reverse the spell.

Chapter Seven

Jamie Discovers More

'I am never, NEVER going to use the spell again.' Jamie wrote in his diary. The swirl covered book which his Gran had presented him with, the day after he had arrived at her house, lay on the desk in front of him. . He had just finished describing the incredible events that had happened after his afternoon in the attic. He was determined to never use the spell again. It had caused him enough trouble already. He turned the cat pendant over in his hand and looked closely at it. This was to be the last time he saw it. He must capture the image in his brain forever. No better still, he would draw it in his diary. He spent several minutes on the task until he was satisfied that he had captured the cat shape and its inscriptions.

Jamie made his way back up the stairs to the attic, making sure that this time he wedged the door open, just in case. He knelt on the dusty floor and opened the box, the treasure box. He had planned to put the pendant back and forget it. As usual, curiosity got the better of him.

"Just one last look at the book." He promised.

Astonished was how Jamie felt, when he examined the remaining pages in the leather-bound, red book. For instead of the hundreds of spells, which he expected, there were none. The other pages were completely blank. He had expected so much more than this, spells and more spells.

Disappointed, Jamie put the book to one side and felt a curious urge to delve further into the box. Inside, he found an untidy pile of other books, each with a cover of a different colour. He picked up the first which was a brown diary. When he opened it, he was amazed to find that on the first page was his name. In bold letters was written, 'Jamie Tyler'. It was his name yet not his handwriting. It was far too fancy to be his. And anyway, he had never seen this book before.

What would he find in here? Whatever it was, it could not be more incredible than what he had already found in the box. Looking more closely at the front cover, Jamie could see that whoever the owner was, he was eleven years old and apparently lived at this address. That was impossible! Only Gran lived here. It must have been someone who lived here way back in the past. When he inspected the diary further, he found that the date on the front page was over fifty years ago. That confirmed it. The diary and the red spell book obviously belonged to someone who had lived in this house in the past.

He decided to ask Gran about the history of the house. Maybe she would know to whom the diary belonged. Maybe she also knew about the box and its contents but surely, if she did, she would have guessed that Jamie had tried the spell when she saw the strange black cat on his bed. Dismissing the questions racing through his mind, he carefully replaced the diary, the red book and the pendant in the box, and closed the lid firmly shut. Never to be opened again, he thought, as a cold shiver ran the length of his spine.

When he got downstairs, Gran was in the kitchen making scones. Both she and Jamie had made a special effort to be kinder to one another since the incident in the attic. He knew she was making the scones for him.

"Gran, who lived in this house before you and Granddad?" he asked.

Gran thought for a moment. It was a strange question.

"Your Granddad's family have lived here for many years. And there was a house belonging to the Tyler family on this site, for a long time before that. Why do you want to know?"

Gran was puzzled and fearful. What was Jamie up to now? But Jamie did not hear Gran's question, nor see the enquiring look on her face, because he was thinking about the books in the attic and who they belonged to. If Granddad had lived in this house all his life, then he must have known the owner of the diary? It didn't occur to him until much later that the owner of the plain brown diary was Granddad himself, that his name had been Jamie too.

Chapter Eight

The Letter

Some days later, back in the attic, Jamie had come to terms with the idea that he was meant to find the box. Granddad meant he should find it. How he knew this, he was not sure but he knew! He opened the box and looked at Granddad's diary again. He picked it up, ready to read about what he was sure were Granddad's adventures with the cat spell. As he pulled the diary out, a white envelope slipped from the back and floated gently to the floor. The envelope had his name on the front.

'To Jamie, My Grandson'

Was this meant for him. He turned the envelope over. It had not been opened. It must be for him. He ripped it open eagerly. This letter could explain everything. Inside there was a single sheet of paper and the writing was like that at the front of the diary. The date at the top of the page was familiar. It most definitely was for him he mused. He read carefully through the letter which his granddad had written especially for him on the day he was born.

Dear Jamie,

By now you will have found the red book. Maybe you have already tried the spell, which is inside. Use it carefully, Jamie. It is a wonderful gift, which has been in our family for many generations but it can be dangerous if used unwisely. My grandfather used it and so did his grandfather before him. You will find, if you look deeper into the box, that the spell has been enjoyed by many Tylers, including me. Some spell, Jamie. Go carefully.

Your Loving Granddad Jim

No way could Jamie seal the box and forget the red book now. His grandfather had given him permission to use it but carefully. So, use it he must. He had a sneaking suspicion that he would have tried it again anyway! Perhaps not straight away but the temptation would have always been there, wouldn't it?

He sat in the attic and imagined all the great tricks he could play using the spell and his imagination ran riot. What fun he could have. What mischief he could cause. All those other Tylers must have had wonderful adventures and marvellous memories of their time with the spell. But how long would the opportunity last? There was no sign that Granddad had used it in the last few years whilst Jamie was around. Was there only a small window of opportunity? A month? A year? Five years? So, why hadn't Granddad told him about it himself? Why write a letter? Was it a secret? Jamie suspected that it was. Perhaps even his grandmother didn't know about it. He whispered into the still of the attic:

"It's our secret, Granddad. I shall never tell until it is time for the next happy magician. It is safe with me, forever until that day." The solemn promise was uttered with absolute truth and absolute certainty.

Jamie looked forward to the weeks ahead when he could try out the spell. Or maybe there weren't weeks left. He must make the most of what time was left, however long that was. And yes, thinking about it, he suspected he would have used the spell again without Granddad's permission. Eventually! Inevitably! Jamie smiled in anticipation.

Chapter Nine

An Afternoon with Granddad

The next afternoon, desperate to use the spell again but needing to know more, Jamie decided to delve further into Granddads diary in the hope of discovering the adventures his grandfather had experienced. He imagined he might find some ideas of how to use the spell, some mischief he could cause. Not that he needed any prompting in causing mayhem. He could figure that out for himself. However, Granddad had some different escapades that he had not thought of. The idea intrigued.

Without delay, Jamie made straight for the door at the head of the extra flight of stairs. Before he pushed it open, he shouted down to Gran,

"Just going to spend some time reading in my room, Gran. Be down later."

Gran, who was ironing a multitude of kaleidoscopic dresses, mumbled a response and continued, only to stop abruptly. She looked out of the open window. The sun was shining brightly and the sky was a beautiful blue. 'Unusual', she thought. 'What is Jamie up to now. Reading NOT fishing'. Strange... Then dismissed it from her mind, singing along , at the top of her voice, to her favourite track.

Jamie was of course oblivious to Gran's thoughts, as he strode purposefully into the attic and opened the box which he had left half hidden behind the mirror. Out of it, he pulled Granddad's diary with a gentle tug and disappeared back to his room to lie on his bed and take it all in.

The first entry in the diary made him laugh.

January 1st, 1940

Hello Diary – It's me Jimmy. Nice to meet you. I'm going to share my adventures with you. Hope you enjoy them.

The next week' was blank as if Granddad Jim had not had any adventures to share. Jamie suspected that his granddad had been given this diary as a Christmas gift and didn't really know what to do with it. However, the next entry he read was more informative:

January 8th 1940

Mum says we've got to start eating less butter, bacon, ham and sugar because the government are rationing it. I don't know what that means

January 9th 1940

Got a letter from Dad today. Still in training. He says he'll be going off to fight soon. I miss him.

Jamie had learned about World War II, rationing and people going off to war, at school last term. It must have been awful. Granddad had never talked about it.

But what about your adventures with the spell, Granddad Jim? When do we get to those? Jamie was impatient. He skipped through several pages of the diary, skimming the contents. There was more about how life had changed for Granddad and his mum but nothing about a spell. When next he stopped to read more carefully, the diary date was four months later:

May 12tth 1940

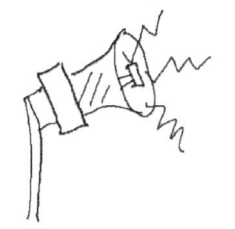

It's awful, diary... The crashing and the wailing, the fire and the sirens. Every night it seems Mum and me go down to the cellar and sit in the darkness until it stops. I hate it.

As the afternoon passed, Jamie began to skim through and pick out entries which looked the most interesting. These often-had simple drawings which his granddad had added to show his feelings.

May 20th 1940

It's still happening, Diary. The next street to ours is just rubble.... Mum says we have to go to the underground station now 'cause its too dangerous in our cellar. I don't want to go. What might we come back to?

35

Jamie thought...'Get on with it Granddad. I know what you saw was bad but surely the spell made things better.' To be fair, Jamie really had no idea how difficult Granddad's life had become: Away from his home every night, hiding and singing in the underground tunnels; Trying desperately to keep cheerful but dreading what might greet them when they ventured out in the morning. Jamie read further:

May 22nd 1940

Oh Diary, Mum says she HAS to go to work at the munitions factory to help with the war effort. She says its too dangerous for me in London now so I've got to go and stop with Granny in the country. I don't want to leave...

June 2nd 1940

I'm waving at mum from the train carriage. Trying not to cry, but she is!

This looked more promising. Jamie soon put to one side the pain in Granddad's words and thought only of the spell, . Was this house where Granddad was going, the house where Jamie was now? He skipped a few more pages and read on.

Chapter Ten

The Interesting Bit

Things had certainly moved on from the last entry. As Jamie read, he knew that he had found what he was looking for:

June 4th 1940

Found the attic at Granny's house. . Wow. Exciting. Lots of boxes and stuff...Will explore tomorrow when Granny is busy. Can't wait.

"Come on Granddad get on with it. Did you find the spell?" Jamie exclaimed impatiently.

June 5th 1940

Found this mysterious looking box in the attic. Spell book inside. Gosh – a spell book no less, diary. Imagine that. So, I tried one...like an idiot I thought it'd work. No flashes, no lights, nothing. Gutted! Woke up later in a daze. Been asleep I think - confused. I dreamt that I was a cat meowing in the dark. A bit scared, Diary. What happened?

'Woah...'. Jamie thought. 'I was disappointed about not seeing flashes or lights too. Curious'.

June 6th 1940

Tried the spell again. Holy Mackerel !!!!! I turned into a grey cat. No kidding, Diary... I saw myself in the mirror. True... I'm going to have such a great time here. Magic... Oh, and Granny is nice too.

Jamie sat back. This was what he was hoping for. He wanted to continue reading but Gran was calling to him from downstairs, so he laid the diary, still open, on his bedside table and went to search for her.

All through tea, Jamie sat quiet, imagining what Granddad was going to write. He was excited. He might find something he could try. Gran assumed that Jamie was upset about not going fishing but then changed her mind. He had chosen not to go. Strange boy. She did not know what went on in his head.

Chapter Eleven

Granddad's Adventures

That evening, Jamie yet again made his excuses and disappeared upstairs to his room. He almost danced his way to his bed and picked up the diary, lifting it into the air like a trophy.

"Come on Granddad…what have you got for me tonight," he whispered as he lay down on the bed, front first, legs waving in the air and the diary on the pillow in front of him. "Let the adventures begin…"

June 7th, 1940, 9.00am.

Well Diary… Back to the spell today. To adventures… Can't wait. Let the adventures begin.

_1.00pm._

Had a great time this this morning, Diary . After turning into the cat – no flashes – or music or stuff like that – shame, I went outside for an adventure. I was just wondering what to do when I spied something moving in the long grass. My cat senses sprung to life; I moved in the direction of something brown scuttling noisily in the undergrowth. A mouse… Don't know why but it popped into my head what fun it would be to chase it, Hahaha. So, I did. Hope Granny doesn't find the broken jam jars in the shed and the bird seed scattered all over the floor. Feel a bit guilty. It was fun though. I jumped and stalked and ran and pawed until the poor thing disappeared

through a hole in the fence. A small hole, I tried to follow but couldn't quite squeeze through. Ah well. Another time.

Jamie smiled. He had felt that urge to chase mice too but as yet, had not given in to it.

Looking back at the diary, he observed two things; How much longer this entry was and how it was written more like a story than just the brief notes of before. It seemed that Granddad had found his voice and a good use for the diary. Then flicking through the next few pages, Jamie noticed a much longer entry a week later. He read on:

June 14th 1940, 9.00am.

Hello again Diary, my friend. Last few days have been MAGIC. Sorry I didn't share much with you but I was too busy having a great time as the grey cat. Yipeeeeeee...

Today I am going to have a marvellously, wonderful adventure. I just know it. I'm off to see Granny, as the cat of course. I've been keeping away from her just in case she knows its me. What the heck... She has this lovely piece of fresh fish; hidden in the larder – yum – She's saving it for her tea. Its my favourite... mmmm. I can just taste it. She says there's not enough for me but I soooooo want some. I'm going to try and get just a little bit... wish me luck.

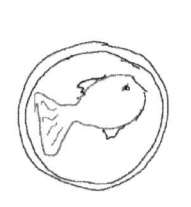

Into battle.

1.30am.

Oh no, Diary, what a stupid boy I am... I've killed Granny!

6.00pm.

Mum is coming to get me soon. I'm at the police station. No not because I **murdered** Granny. She's ok. After I spoke to you last, I heard Granny whimpering and when I went to look at her, she WASN'T dead!.

I ran as fast as I could to Doctor Jones' house. and he came with his bag and that funny thing he wears round his neck. He examined Granny and then took her to the hospital in town. A policeman just told me that she's broken her ankle and banged her head...She will need to stay there for a while. Relieved. Also worried. What will Mum say?

8.00pm.

Mum's arrived from London. The police officer explained to her that Granny had tripped over a cat that was trying to steal her fish from the larder. Mum is saying not very nice things about that cat... about me! Guilty as charged. Ashamed.

June 14th 1940, 9.00am.

Home - - in London. Miserable...

Jamie put down the diary. For a minute there, he thought that his Granddad had actually killed someone. No adventure was worth that...

Enough reading for now. Perhaps there were more adventures in Granddad's diary but he doubted it. There was no mention of taking the spell back to London with him. Jamie couldn't blame Granddad. What an awful time he must have endured thinking he'd killed his own Grandmother. No, Jamie didn't think there would be any more adventures of the grey cat, even though there were still plenty of pages unread in the diary. Perhaps he would look at those another day. For now, he wanted to try out the spell himself.

"Oh and I'll try hard not to kill anyone..." he laughed loudly then suddenly became serious.

Chapter Twelve

House-Breaking, TV Treat and Stuck Up a Tree

From that day on, Jamie used the spell, for nothing momentous, just fun. Being careful NOT to trip his Gran up like his Granddad had done ... accidently of course. He had read through some of the eight other diaries in the box but had not returned to that of his granddad. It seemed that all his ancestors had used the spell just for fun, nothing too daring, and nothing too dangerous. Until the final time. Right from the first, James, the tiler's son, there had been little harm in what they had used the spell for. That is until the final event. Incredibly, all the spell users were named James or Jim or Jamie. The family name? They had all found the spell book when they were eleven years old. They had all felt compelled to use it, as Jamie had. He recalled his adventures up to date with amusement.

The spell had been most useful on several occasions. There was the time when he and Gran had been shopping, to return and find themselves locked out of the house. The door key, of course was safely locked inside the cabinet in the kitchen. Gran wanted to call the police or the fire brigade, Jamie assured her that he could get into the house without their help. He knew a small window at the back of the was open. He had seen it that morning before they left. He just needed to find a secluded spot in which to use the five magic words and the pendant. Finding it quickly and quietly, he changed himself with the spell and made straight for the open window.

Luckily, Gran did not see the black cat, as it crept in through the window. However, she was both happy and surprised to see Jamie open the front door to her minutes later. His, 'I told you I could do it', made her smile and wonder what sort of tricks he had learned since she had seen him last holidays. She told him that she did not understand how he had managed this 'miracle' and that maybe she didn't really WANT to know, but that he surely was extremely clever and resourceful! That night, she made him his favourite tea as a thank you. Jamie was very glad that he had thought to use the spell. Not only had he had fun, balancing on the window ledge, and climbing in through the window, but he had managed to secure a rather large portion of chocolate ice-cream as well. He smiled like the cat that had got the cream which he certainly was!

On another occasion, Jamie had wanted to watch a late-night space adventure on the television. It started at ten o'clock and finished very late. He argued non-stop with Gran for half an hour, before he realised that she would not give in and let him watch. Just like their arguments about riding the motor bike, he thought. He slumped in his room, sad and annoyed, until he remembered the spell. What an opportunity. With a little daring and a lot of luck, he could watch the film and Gran would be none the wiser.

At nine o'clock precisely, he took out the pendant from its hiding place and murmured the five magic words. There was no flash, which was still disappointing but what did that matter, the adventure awaited. Downstairs, Gran let the now familiar black cat she had christened Sweep, settle on the armchair, as she switched on the TV to enjoy the film. Jamie enjoyed it too. Not that Gran knew that. Well, not yet anyway.

However, this escapade had two quite tricky moments. Firstly, after the film had finished, Gran insisted on giving her newfound feline friend a saucer of milk. This proved difficult as Jamie tried hard to lap up the milk, but most of it ended up on the floor or lying very stickily around his whiskers! It was almost as difficult as looking at the world and particularly the TV screen, through cat's eyes.

Secondly, the following day, Gran stood talking to Jamie about the film.

"It was so sad when the astronaut died," she said.

Jamie did not agree, telling Gran that he deserved it for being stupid enough to take off his helmet when he didn't know if there was enough air to breathe. Just for a moment, Jamie thought he had got away with his mistake. Then, Gran stared at him with steely eyes:

"How do YOU know what happened, young man?" she asked very quietly. Jamie knew this meant trouble. He smiled.

"Erm, well... I've seen it before, Gran!" Weak, Jamie, but it was all that he had,

It was the best he could do, on the spur of the moment. Fortunately, Gran chose to believe his excuse. However, he suspected that she thought he had crept down, late last night and watched the film through the open living room door. Jamie smiled again; little did she know. That was close.

A third occasion saw Jamie being a little more adventurous with the spell. He wanted to see what was happening in the garden next door to Gran's. Interesting noises were coming from that direction and curiosity took hold. He could have gone round and asked if he could investigate, of course, but he knew that Gran's neighbours weren't very friendly towards children, so he decided to use the spell and climb a tree to see 'first paw' what was happening.

It all went well, to begin with. Jamie changed shape quickly and scaled the heady height of the tall oak tree in Gran's Garden. All went well that is, until he looked down. Whoa, he hadn't realise he'd come this high. He wasn't afraid of heights exactly; it was just that he didn't like having his feet that far off the ground. That's why he didn't like flying. Why he thought it would be different, if he were a cat, he did not know but it wasn't. He got that same dizzy, sickly feeling, he always got. Oh help! What to do now? Well, he couldn't meow, he thought. That would change him back. If he fell, he stood a better chance of landing on his feet as a cat than as a boy. Cats do land on their feet or so they say. Oh help!

Just at that moment, something distracted Jamie's attention away from holding on tightly and to his horror his back feet, no paws, slipped and left him dangling in empty space. Digging his front paw nails in, he desperately tried to think what to do next. Fortunately,

Gran came out of the back door in time to see the black cat scrabbling back onto the branch. For several minutes, she tried to coax the frightened animal down from the narrow branch. Seeing that this was useless however, she decided to ring the fire brigade. There was no-one to persuade her otherwise, this time.

A wiry-looking fireman arrived shortly and smiled at the old lady and her distressed pet. In no time, the ladder was collected, and the fireman was in amongst the branches. Imagine Jamie's embarrassment, as the fireman took a bag from his pocket, bundled Jamie into it and carried him to safety. However, embarrassment disappeared as Jamie thought of his narrow escape. Besides which the bag had given him an idea. But that was for later when he returned home.

Chapter Thirteen
Gran's Plan

And so the summer progressed. Jamie DID occasionally go fishing but it had lost its charm in the face of his cat adventure. Gran had adopted the stray black cat and spent many a night with it nestled on her lap, watching her favourite films on TV. Jamie enjoyed those films too...well most of them anyway. Gran did like romances rather a lot but she also liked adventure, and sci-fi and westerns. Jamie loved the little treats too, creamy milk, steamed fish but drew a line at the cat food Gran tried to feed him! She had no inkling that the cat was indeed Jamie and just assumed he was fishing or in bed when she spent time with Sweep.

Today, 'Sweep' lay on the grass, basking in the sun whilst Gran sat on her stripey deckchair, reading. Jamie thought life could get no better. 'These were the days. Just living the dream.' he thought sleepily.

Suddenly Gran jumped to her feet, dropped her magazine to the floor and shrieked....

"What a great idea..." Jamie half asleep jumped up in fright, claws untethering, hackles rising. "Its ok, Sweep. Nothing to worry about," she soothed but her voice was still excited. Little did Jamie know that it was EVERYTHING to worry about, so he settled down back into his slumbers.

He was to find out later, to his horror, what the great idea was and the plan Gran had put into action. Transformed back into Jamie, they were sitting at the kitchen table, eating tea, when Gran dropped her bombshell.

"So, you know this cat I've adopted Jamie," she began. He was sure she was going to go through all the funny antics the black cat had been up to. He went along with this even though he knew it all. It was a game he played, acknowledging this charade without offering any comment.

"Yes, Gran." He smiled."

"And you know I was reading the church magazine this morning,"

'Where is all this going?' thought Jamie, only half listening.

Well, It's the village fete next week, and I've entered Sweep into the cat show," Gran stated, with a huge grin on her face, clapping her hands gleefully. !"He's so handsome...."

"You've done WHAT!" shouted Jamie, jumping to his feet to a loud scraping of his chair over the stone floor. .

"Why so upset Jamie? Are you jealous of a little pussy cat?" Gran joked.

"Of course not, Gran, but are you sure? He might belong to someone there and then you'll have to give him up,"

"That's fine," replied Gran, "Then he'll go home with his family..."

Jamie spent an exhausting hour trying, no begging Gran to change her mind but she was adamant. Whatever reason he put forward; she stood her ground. What was he going to do? How was he going to cope? He thought about just not using the spell on that day. No good. Gran would be so upset; He could tell that she was looking forward to it so much. Jamie also knew that she had entered every possible competition at the fete and never won once. And she was so sure this time that she would win first prize. But how would he cope? He hated being the centre of attention.

Jamie spent the next few days veering between convincing Gran that the Cat Show was NOT a good idea and just accepting that it would happen. Should he risk upsetting her and forget the spell or should he run away disguised as a cat. Both ideas were unthinkable. Both would upset Gran deeply and he didn't want that. Finally, he accepted that the show was going to happen and he was going to be part of it. Granddad had warned him to be careful. Is this what he meant?

Chapter Fourteen
The Village Fete

The day of the fete arrived, and Jamie reluctantly eased himself out of bed, slowly washing and dressing himself for the day. Gran was singing tunelessly down in the kitchen, as she made breakfast. 'She's obviously happy' Jamie thought begrudgingly. I'm not.' He thought of the day ahead. Of the crowds of people staring at him. Of the judges inspecting every part of his cat body. Of Gran's disappointment when she did not win... He ambled down the stairs and into the kitchen, a scowl painted clearly on his face.

"What's up with you, sourpuss?" Gran said as she looked at his face. Well of course it was the wrong thing to say, and Jamie's scowl deepened,

"Nothing..." he mumbled, sitting down to eat his breakfast. Gran, seeing that he was in no mood for chat, kept silent and quickly moved to thinking about the fete, excitement apparent in both her face and her movements. Jamie finished his breakfast quickly and with a wave of his hand, disappeared off to the river to fish. Or so his grandmother thought as she vaguely acknowledged his 'Bye'.

Once in his room, Jamie put on the pendant and whispered the simple words; there was still no flashing lights as he transformed into Sweep, but he witnessed it all in the mirror. First a small black triangle appeared in the middles of his face, quickly followed by the sprouting of long wiry whiskers at each side. At the same time, his eyes slanted and turned a beautiful emerald green. Soon his body bent of its own accord and as his hands touched the floor his back arched and a swirling tail appeared. Finally, hands and feet changed to delicate paws as jet black hair sprung up out all over his body. What happened to his clothes, Jamie did not know but they appeared again when he transformed back 'Well it is magic,' he thought, padding out of the room and back downstairs.

Oh, the indignity of it all. The embarrassment. Gran had spent the last few hours bathing and combing his fur, spraying fowl smelling perfume on it until Jamie could bear it no more. He squirmed and wriggled until Gran finally let go of the collar, she had made him wear. .Free for a moment, he sprang from the kitchen table and headed for the back door. Oh, how he wished for the spell to have been lost or not working so he did not find himself in this situation.

Should he change back? That really was not an option, so he gritted his feline teeth and halted mid escape.

"Oh no, little pussycat. I've not finished with you yet," Gran chuckled as she scooped him back on to the table. "The final touch....Ta...da".

It was then that she produced the final insult, a shiny blue ribbon which she carefully tied in a disgustingly big bow around his neck.

Pleased with that finishing touch, Gran disappeared, leaving Jamie to wonder if cats could scowl - because if they could, then he surely was. She returned to the kitchen where she placed a large cardboard box, holes dotted around the top, onto the table next to a bemused Jamie, . What now? …………Oh no. You are NOT putting me in that! Gran had other ideas. She opened the lid and before Jamie could run, she had picked him up and was attempting to force him into the box. A lot of hissing and scratching and tail swinging later, Jamie was safely inside, the lid firmly shut. Imprisoned…

Ten minutes later, Jamie felt the weird sensation of being swung from side to side, his body crashing into the cardboard of the box in a gentle rhythm. .He heard Gran whistling as she put the box in the back of her battered old car. He would never forget the next 15 minutes for as long as he lived. Gran drove with speed, careless of the precious cargo in her boot. Jamie was thrown hither and thither with regular, bruising, motion as she swerved around corners until she suddenly stopped with the screech of old brakes. Jamie ended up in a heap in an upside-down box. No more, his body cried but he knew he had to see this through.

It seemed like hours later that Jamie was still locked in a wire cage where his Gran had bundled him. She had put a pink blanket inside and attached a card label on the door, bearing the name Sweep. Then she had disappeared. It looked as if she skipped away. Jamie tried to sleep, lying on the blanket, but as he started to doze a sea of childish faces appeared, staring at him, giggling and prodding him through the wire. It was useless hissing at them, it just made them do it more. It reminded him of 'Bad Billy'. More faces , adults and children paced passed his prison. Admiring, condemning, and talking about his chance of winning. Jamie hated being the centre of attention. Misery.

Finally, three smart looking men approached his enclosure. The Judges...One opened the cage door and pulled Jamie unceremoniously out and placed him on a wooden table, try to stand still, Jamie. It'll be over soon. They pulled and prodded him, stretched his neck, lifted his legs and muttered. However, the final straw came when a ruddy looking face pushed itself at Jamie, lifted his tail and stared at his bottom! Well really. This was enough!

Jamie fought with all his might, legs flying, claws scratching, mouth hissing until the judges jumped back in alarm. Freedom. He bounded off in search of a place to hide, chased by the three judges who tried to stop his progress. He found his way under the flap of a large tent, backing his way in. keeping a keen lookout for the judges. They seemed to have given up the chase.

Then Jamie heard a piercing shriek...

"What's that cat doing in the food tent? Shoo, you horrible beast. Get out!" A tall, slim, cross looking woman headed towards him.' Not likely. You are not catching me and taking me back,' thought Jamie. He jumped up onto a table filled to overflowing all manner of food, beautifully displayed ready to be judged. The woman stretched grasping hands towards him. Mistake. Jamie turned ready to flee, tail swishing from side to side in anger. Plates, cakes, pies and pastries flew in all directions as the tall woman tried to extract Jamie from amongst them. Jars of jam crashed to the floor, dishes of nuts and seeds scattered in untidy heaps on the table. She could not catch the wretched cat.

At that moment Gran walked into the tent wanting to see what all the commotion was about. She saw Jamie. She saw the mess and thought a speedy retreat would be in order. With one sweep of her arms, she scooped him up and bundled him into her shopping bag.

"You naughty boy, Sweep," she muttered, looking around at the mayhem he had caused. Her face pink with embarrassment, she made a hasty exit and without looking back shoved her bag and Jamie into the car and drove off. Jamie thought it best to lay still. Oh, if only the ground would open up and swallow him. Would Gran ever forgive him.

Chapter Fifteen
Granddad's Warning

After the incident at the fete, Jamie decided two things. He would not use the spell for a while, and he must lay low. Gran had not forgiven Sweep... not yet. The rain outside fell in torrents so fishing was out of the question. What should he do? Quickly the thought of reading the rest of Granddad's adventures came to him. The diary still lay open on his bedside table, so he picked it up and resumed the position front down on the bed.

He read again the last entry in the book:

June 14th 1940, 9.00am.

Home - - in London. Miserable...

Jamie was sure he would find no more adventures after Granddad's unfortunate incident with his grandmother, but he continued, hoping he would find out more about war torn London. However, as he flicked through, there were only blank pages and Jamie thought that Granddad had given up on the diary altogether. What a disappointment. Then several pages later the entries started again.

July 20th, 1940.

Hello Diary. Sorry I've not been here in a while. It's awful, So scared. Bombs are falling EVERY night. Sometimes two or three land by our house. Mum and I are still going to the underground tunnel. We're so tired. And diary....not used the spell since you know....Gran.

Jamie was right.

July 25th 1940.

Evening Diary... so I was out today, minding my own business when I heard something crying from one of the bombed-out houses. - tried to find someone to tell but couldn't see anyone, not even the Warden. So I peered into a hole in the rubble and I could see a baby... no kidding.... A REAL baby. I tried to squeeze in to get her but I'm too big! Then I had a thought....What If? I had the pendant in my pocket. So I did - I changed into the cat...no flashes...It was easy to get through the hole and I managed to pull the baby out by her blanket. Changed back. Got help. I'm a HERO., Diary, a BLOOMIN' H-E-R-O.

July 28th, 1940

Well Diary...Mum is still talking about her brave little boy...me. I'm loving it. I got extra rations... Little does she know.

August 15th 1940

On this day, in place of Granddad's writing there was a folded newspaper clipping Jamie carefully opened it up and read.

Lucky the Cat Strikes Again

The new sensation, Lucky the Cat has been on the prowl again, saving folks from certain death.

Jamie's eyes widened. He skimmed the newspaper article. A grey cat that had been christened Lucky by the 'folks in the local area' had been saving lives by rescuing those trapped under the rubble of bombed houses. People said that if you were trapped and saw a grey cat you were lucky... The cat had saved a number of lives of both woman and children, and all were extremely grateful. However, no one knew where the cat had come from and when they looked for it afterwards it could never be found. What a mystery. The article went on to list quotes from the public where words like 'dodging danger ', 'godsend' and 'hero' were used.

Underneath the cutting, Granddad had written in big bold letters. THAT'S ME! Jamie was impressed...

The next pages were filled with more rescues and it was clear that Granddad was bathing in his own glory. Jamie thought that Granddad Jim seemed to be getting a little bit big-headed about it. The more rescues, the bigger the word HERO was scrawled in the diary. In fact, on some pages that's all that was written.

"Oh Granddad Jim. Mum always says pride comes before a fall.... Didn't you remember what nearly happened to your own Gran? "

As Jamie read on, it seemed that Granddad HAD forgotten. Jamie threw down the diary, not wishing to read anymore. As he did so, another newspaper cutting fell out. He opened it and stared at a photo of a girl about the same age as him, holding a grey cat in her arms. The caption read Rosie Garner and Lucky. He knew that the girl was Gran and the cat was Granddad. The headline proclaimed:

Lucky Escape

Jamie almost dismissed the article as another one of granddad's now familiar recues but the header caught his eye and made him read on.

Famous recue cat Lucky is rescued by Rosie. Both are LUCKY to be alive.

Jamie's attention was captured. Reading on, he discovered that this time Lucky had squeezed into an old factory and was followed by Rosie. When interviewed, she said that she just wanted to help the cat and be a hero too. Both had been trapped by falling debris and would surely have died if a passing warden had not heard Rosie's shouts. As for the cat, he had been knocked clean out. The warden had blown his whistle and the fire brigade had been called from a nearby phone box. It had taken several nerve-wracking hours to make the building safe and bring the two to safety. Rosie, badly bruised and the still dazed cat were 'snapped' by the waiting photographers as they and their rescuers emerged to a round of applause from the watching crowd.

"Not such a hero after all, eh Granddad Jim," Jamie murmured aloud. "Mum says pride ALWAYS comes before a fall."

There were no more entries in the diary.

Jamie decided to take one last look at the letter written by Granddad on the day he was born before he put both back into the attic. Picking up the envelope and taking out the paper inside, Jamie was surprised to see something else written on the back. It said.

'PS You've probably read all of the diary and newspaper clippings, Jamie. You now see how dangerous this spell can be if you get carried away with it and your own importance. I not only nearly killed my own Granny with it but nearly killed your Gran too. I shudder to think of what would have become of me if that had happened. So take care with the spell, my beautiful grandson. Use it wisely.

GJ'

Chapter Sixteen
Jamie's Plan

It was the last day at Gran's house, when Jamie realised two things. Firstly, the holiday had not been at all the sort he expected. Surprisingly, he had not missed fishing at all. . There had been no time for anything except the spell.. All thoughts and actions tied up in the box in the attic. It had become an obsession.

This certainly wasn't the holiday I expected it to be, Gran," he said when they were talking on the last day of his stay. Gran sympathised.

"No, you haven't been able to do much fishing, have you, Jamie," she replied, still slightly bemused by the fact that Jamie had not gone to the river even on some of those few fine weather days.

"It has been terrible weather!"

Gran was not to know that this was not quite what Jamie meant. His second discovery, however, could not be discussed with Gran so he went to his room to think more about it.

Jamie concluded that the small adventures which he had enjoyed with the spell were not nearly enough. He wanted more. He knew greater things were possible, more important things. And if he took care to heed Granddad's warning, all would be well. He began to think of what he could do that would be the adventure to outdo all the others. Jamie was a brave boy, daring; he could do anything he wanted with the spell. It was his after all, his grandfather had told him so. There was also the idea with the bag that had flashed through his mind during the tree rescue. That was it! He hit upon the plan almost immediately, as if it had been there in the back of his mind all along. It required daring and bravery. It seemed right that such a gift should be used to seek revenge upon his greatest enemy. Not only revenge for himself but for all the other boys at his school. No, not revenge but justice.

He thought back to the early days of the holiday. He thought about the day he had found the box in the attic. He thought how he had so very nearly sealed the red book in that box, forever. It was too late to regret anything now. Once thought, the plan must be carried out. He sighed. Would Granddad approve? Would the others? He pushed these disturbing thoughts to the back of his mind and began to plan his new adventure, the one to outdo all others.

This new plan MUST work. He must decide upon every tiny little detail, before beginning. It had to work. No mistakes and unfortunate accidents like Granddad had endured. Doubts filled his mind. What would his grandfather say? The same things went round his head, over and over again. Nothing quite like this had ever been attempted before. Could he, do it? Could he pull it off? No time for questions because now it was time for action. Things had gone on too long. Things had gone too far. He must put it right, immediately. Here in his hands, he had the ideal opportunity to bring about justice. He put aside his doubts and began to plan the perfect plan. Watch out, Billy! Jamie smiled.

Chapter Seventeen
Preparations

Of course, putting the new plan into action had to wait until Jamie was back home. It involved some careful preparations and a certain amount of luck. Jamie had it all mapped out in his mind. He had waited a long time for this day. He had waited a long time for this opportunity. He would not let anything go wrong.

It was while Jamie was putting the finishing touches to the preparations, that he realised his plan had one major flaw; If the spell only worked\d at his grandmother's house then his treasured plan would not work. How would he get Billy to Gran's? Don't be ridiculous, he thought, I'd never get him there. Jamie felt deflated, defeated before he had begun. His wonderful plan could fail at the first hurdle! What could he do? He would NOT give up the plan! It worked in London for Granddad Jim.

After careful thought, Jamie realised that he needed to try the spell here, where he had decided to wreak his revenge. But what could he do? Ding! The solution swept into his head. He smiled and thought of Luke. This could be fun as well as the answer to his question. Luke was visiting that afternoon. He could witness Jamie's transformation in person. Well maybe not exactly.

Luke arrived ten minutes later. Jamie was waiting.

"Want to play computer games? Jamie asked, before Luke had even stepped through the door.

"OK," Luke replied. "We'll play Demon House." Luke named his favourite game, as Jamie knew he would. He always won. Jamie didn't stand a chance, not unless he cheated. Jamie smiled. Oh well, he'll get over it.

The game was soon set up and Luke made his usual brilliant start, dodging and diving, playing the demons at their own game. Jamie didn't stand a chance!

"You know you're not to look now, while I hide my secret weapon," Luke said. "Go out of the room, while I do it. You won't win, of course!" Luke laughed. Jamie bounced out of the room.

"Wanna bet!," Jamie shouted over his shoulder.

In the hallway, Jamie quickly looked around, but no-one was there. He could hear Mum in the kitchen, singing a catchy song she'd heard in Jamaica. He felt the pendant around his neck. He said the words. Still no flash, but there to his relief, in the mirror, he saw his alter ego, one very pleased black cat. Sweep. He strolled back into the living room, just in time to see Luke hide the secret weapon. Gotcha!

Luke thought the cat was a bit of a nuisance, jumping on his knee, getting in the way, spoiling his concentration. He shooed it down several times, picking it up and dropping it to the ground with a thud. Jamie didn't mind, he just kept annoying Luke. He not only wanted to win but to win in style. And if Luke was annoyed, he was unlikely to notice Jamie's winning moves. However, he soon got bored with these antics and retreated once again to the hall, where he changed back to normal.

Walking back into the room, Jamie was not surprised by the cross look on Luke's face.

"Didn't know you'd got a cat. What a nuisance! It kept jumping up and spoiling my concentration. Luke complained. "I'll still win though"

"What cat? We don't have a cat, must be your imagination!" Jamie replied. The game continued; the cat forgotten. Jamie bided his time, looking as if he was going to lose. Luke continued to play brilliantly. The last battle was underway. The demons in the game fought bravely but Luke was better. Jamie's game was good, but not inspired until....

"Time for your secret weapon, I think," shouted Jamie, retrieving it from Luke's hiding place. Luke was stunned.

"How'd you know where that was? Did you cheat? Did you look while I was hiding it?"

"Careful thought and a bit of luck," Jamie laughed. "You're slipping, Luke. Told me where it was yourself."

Luke did not understand and probably never would. Nevertheless, Jamie hadn't the heart to go on and beat him. He let him win but Luke had been given a shock, Jamie had found out that the spell worked here and all was as it should be. Jamie smiled. Poor Luke. Not so poor Billy.

Chapter Eighteen
The Revenge Begins

Before leaving his grandmother's house, Jamie had taken one last look at the red book. He had carefully written down the five words on a piece of scrap paper. He had sat in the attic and called out loud:

"Wish me luck, Granddad. Wish me luck all you other Tylers in the attic. This time the spell will be used to do some good. If it works maybe my school will be a safer place."

And in the quiet of the attic, Jamie thought he heard voices coming down through the ages, spurring him on, giving him their approval for what he was about to do,

Now, Jamie was back home. He had been here just two days. The trick with Luke was fading into the background as he realised that it was now possible to put his plan into action. The cat pendant lay heavily around his neck. It was one of the most important parts of his plan. The pendant must show!

The next day, on his way to the post office to collect stamps for his mother, Jamie saw the person he most wanted to meet, coming towards him. Strange, the one person he usually tried to avoid was now the one person he desperately wanted to see. To add to his perfect enjoyment, Jamie noticed that Mouse was not with Billy today.

Before leaving home, he had taken the big bag, his mother used for pegs. It was ready for action. Perhaps he knew his chance would come today. He had the bag stuffed firmly into his coat pocket.

"Nice to see ya, Jellyboy!" Billy jeered.

Jamie cringed. He hated that name.

Did you have good holiday with granny?" Bad Billy Braithwaite scoffed

"Went fishin', didn't we. Pity the weather was bad. I'm really sorry, Jellyboy!"

It was obvious, Billy was not sorry at all. Jamie willed Billy to look at the pendant. His plan would not work unless he did. Jamie touched it with his finger, not daring to breathe, lest Billy should see how nervous he was.

The pendant winked, wickedly in the sunlight. Billy could not help but notice it. He stared at it. He wanted it.

"I see you've brought me a pressie off your hols, Jellyboy. Give it here now, so's I can try it on for size!"

Jamie knew Billy wanted the pendant. He was staring right at it. Jamie hid his smile.

"This old thing, Billy? You don't want this!"

"Give it here, Jamie and do as your told!"

Billy Braithwaite held out his hand and Jamie placed the pendant into it. Billy turned the pendant over in his sweaty palm. In the light shining off the metal, he could have sworn he saw his name. He put it on with a gleam of triumph in his eyes. If only he had bothered to look, he would have seen the same gleam mirrored in Jamie's.

Billy was about to go... And take the pendant with him. Jamie stopped him with a shout:

"Oh Billy. Don't go. Could you read these words for me? Please. I can't read them and I know how good YOU are at reading. They'll be really easy for you." Jamie used his most whining, pleading voice. "Please, Billy. I did bring you a present." Jamie knew full well that Billy found reading hard but refused to admit it.

Billy turned. He was suspicious but he could not resist the flattery. He looked closely at Jamie. Perhaps he would show this stupid boy how much better he was at reading.

"O.K Jelly, I know I can read them. Give them to me. I can see your no good at reading." Billy sniggered. What a fool Jamie was. Billy looked at the words. He had forgotten that Jamie was good at EVERYTHING as he stood blinded by a little flattery and recognition.

" What are they for, eh. Have you gotta learn them for school. I don't know whether I should help." He remembered all the time that Jamie had tried to help him. Now it was his turn to make Jamie look foolish.

Billy had not changed his mind, but he could not resist tormenting Jamie. What a wimp! He snatched the piece of paper from Jamie's hand, and read the words out loud in a bored voice:

"Magic.....

Invades.....

All....

Our.....

Worlds....!"

Jamie looked on with satisfaction as he saw 'Bad Billy Braithwaite' change into an enormous, sour-faced ginger tomcat.

Before Billy could grasp that something had changed, Jamie drew the peg bag from his pocket and bundled a spitting Billy into it. The first part of the plan was over and had been successful. Now for step two. Jamie hoped that the rest of the plan would be as successful.

Chapter Nineteen

Mouse's Turn

Jamie could see the house, where Mouse lived, quite clearly from the corner of the street. Billy was safely tied in the peg bag and Jamie had only to wait until Mouse returned from whatever mischief he was up to. While he waited, Jamie went over the next part of his plan.

Most people assumed that Mouse had been given his nickname because he was the exact opposite of a mouse. He was big and rough, not small and timid. Jamie knew better. Jamie knew that Mouse had been given his name because he was scared of cats. And what did Jamie have in his bag? He had a very puzzled and definitely very bad-tempered cat in his bag. Here was the cat with the cunning of 'Bad Billy Braithwaite'. Here was the cat that had the temper and malice of 'Bad Billy'. Here in the peg bag was Jamie's revenge! Jamie smiled at the thought of what would happen, when the cat and Mouse met. It was certain to be explosive. Soon they would find out.

It was not long before Mouse came lumbering down the street and into his house. He did not notice Jamie on the corner, waiting for him. That was good. Jamie was sure he was doing the right thing, as he walked up the path to the front door,

"See how THEY like being picked on," he told no-one in particular.

Jamie knew that although he would be afraid, Mouse was sure to put up a good fight. He knew, also, that Billy would find out quickly what had happened, even if he did not understand, and that he would take advantage of the situation. AND enjoy it!

Jamie knocked on the door. He politely asked Mouses mum if he could see her son and he was shown into the living room. Mouse was playing with his new computer game. Demon House, Jamie noticed with amusement. As soon as his mother left the room, Mouse questioned Jamie.

"What do you want here Jamie. Have you come back for that kick?"

Jamie quickly stepped away from Mouse, as he lifted his foot to deliver the kick.

"I've brought you a present back from my holidays, Mouse. I hope you like it."

With that, he let Billy out of the bag. Jamie almost laughed aloud at Mouses' face. It was nearly as funny as the look in Billy's eyes when he caught sight of himself in the mirror.

What followed was a mystery to Jamie because he didn't stay to see the outcome. There was sure to be a good scrap but Jamie wasn't stupid enough to stay and get caught up in it. He crept silently out of the room, just as cat and boy were eyeing up each other, ready for the 'kill'. Jamie heard Mouses' mum as she busied herself in the kitchen. He hoped that she would not realise what was going on, until the two bullies had learned their lesson. Jamie smiled in anticipation.

As he walked home, Jamie continued to grin. Hopefully, when the two had made a good fight of it, and Billy had discovered how to turn himself back, they might think about the way they treated others. Well, that was the plan anyway. And if it did not work? It served them both right to be on the receiving end for a change.

Chapter Twenty

Billy's Caught and Mouse is Taught a Lesson

It was apparent the next morning that things had not gone exactly to plan. When he heard the whole story, however, Jamie was more than satisfied with the unexpected result. It seemed that there had been an exceptionally good fight between Mouse and Billy, lots of scratches, bruises and breakages.

Luke could not contain his excitement as he told Jamie the amazing story: Mouses' mum alerted by the awful noise and sound of breaking glass, had discovered the mayhem in the living room, caused by the cat and her son. She had immediately called the R.S.P.C.A. They had arrived and after much chasing, cornering and more breakages, they had caught the ginger cat and taken him to the local cattery for strays.

Jamie could not believe this lucky turn of events. It served Billy right, he told himself. He deserved to be locked up all night! Mouse apparently had been grounded by his furious dad, for a whole month. He was allowed to go out only to school when the new term began but was expected to return by a certain time. With a bit of luck, Billy would have seen sense and persuaded Mouse not to come after Jamie, by then. Mouse had been made to clear up all the mess as well and pay for the damages out of his pocket money. Served him right.

However, the best was yet to come. Later that day, Jamie had a visit from 'Bad Billy' himself. He turned up at Jamie's house, the evil gleam seemingly gone from his eye. It had been replaced with one of respect and, yes, fear. The story that he told Jamie showed that justice had been done. Billy had realised who had been responsible for changing him into a cat. He did not understand how or why this was. He begged Jamie to tell the police everything. Jamie refused, saying,

"They wouldn't believe me, Billy. You see what your bad ways have got you into?" Billy stepped away from Jamie. He was obviously too afraid to continue. He secretly thought Jamie was a wizard who could do who knew what.

"Please, Jamie. Don't do it to me again. I promise I won't be rotten to you. And I'll tell Mouse to leave you alone too." Billy stood head down, small whimpers leaving his lips. It reminded Jamie of the old Billy,

This was too good an opportunity to miss. Jamie made Billy promise that he would not hurt anyone in the future and that he would see to it that Mouse didn't either. When Billy told Jamie of the events of the previous night, it was clear that he was afraid of not only Jamie, but of the police too.

Billy explained that he had been taken to the cat's home and been put into a cage with a very snooty Persian. His 'cell mate' was obviously a pedigree, worth thousands. Billy had spent several hours thinking about what had happened and had sworn to himself that he would never be bad again, if only he could get out. If only the nightmare would end! He was scared that Jamie would keep him bewitched forever, locked in a cage or worse still at the mercy of some horrible kid, who wanted to 'look after' him   If only he could escape from this cage and from this skin he would be GOOD! Promise.

That was not the end. Feeling miserable in his prison, Billy had done the very same thing that Jamie had done in the attic. He cried for help. The girl in charge arrived to see what all the noise was about, to find Billy, returned to his usual self, locked in the cage with the expensive Persian. She suspected that he was up to no good and despite his pleas and bizarre explanation, had called the police. They had questioned Billy thoroughly and for a very long time.:

"I tried to tell them that I didn't know 'ow I'd got there and I wasn't tryin' to pinch that stupid cat. Even the nice lady who came in with me didn't believe me. I could see it in 'er eyes, Jamie. What could I tell 'em," whimpered Billy, brushing away what looked suspiciously like a tear. "They wouldn't have believed me!"

Jamie could not help a small smile. He tried to hide it and succeeded. Almost. The police were going to keep a close eye on Billy for a long time. Even if Billy had thought to break his promise, they would make sure he kept to the straight and narrow. Poor Billy Braithwaite. Jamie smiled. He'd get over it.

Chapter Twenty-One
The Truth

The pendant was lost. There was no doubt about it. Jamie was quite sure that Billy was telling the truth when he said he could not find it. The spell was finished, forever. Jamie thought it had done some good anyway. But no-one else would ever use it again. Pity.

On the way with his mum to his grandmother's house for a day's visit, Jamie promised himself one last look in the box, in the attic. One last read through the other diaries. He clutched his own in his hands. He had written in here about all his adventures, the large and the small, the insignificant and the far-reaching. He would put his diary in the box with the others. Perhaps, one day, someone like him would find them and enjoy reading about the spell, although it was no longer there to use.

In the dusty attic, he opened the box with care.

"For the very last time," he whispered.

The red book was there, on the top, as usual. The eight coloured diaries snuggled neatly underneath. He opened the red book and looked at the pages. Although he scanned everyone carefully, he could find no record of the spell. The book was completely empty. The spell too was lost. It had disappeared. The book was blank! With sadness, he carefully placed his diary on top of the others but as yet did not put back the red book. He did not know why.

Jamie was devastated. He was the one responsible for losing the spell forever. He had lost the pendant. It was all his fault. He began to think that this had happened because he had used the spell to take revenge, to wreak misery on another. He knew this was so. Maybe it was not meant to be used in such a way. None of the others had been quite so daring, quite so…… vindictive. Jamie lay down the red book and sighed. His sadness filled the room. Would the others forgive him? Then, he could not resist a last look at his grandfather's diary. Perhaps Granddad could help him? He thought that if he held the diary in his hand for one last time, he might in some way be able to apologise for his stupidity.

As he picked it up, another much smaller letter fell again from the last page. One last look. One last link with his granddad. He took out the paper from the envelope and read . As he did, he remembered Granddads words: 'Use the spell carefully', he had said, but he had not. It was lost forever. Jamie did not know what made him turn over the paper but, as he did so, he saw, to his surprise, that there was something scribbled on the back. It read:-

P.S. Jamie. It seems that you must be the last to use this spell. I'm sorry that we cannot go on using it. I have found today, another book. In it there is a message for us all to take notice of. Look under the false bottom of the box, and you will know as much as I.

Granddad xxx

Jamie took out the diaries and found to his amazement that, when he pulled at the bottom of the box, it slid away to reveal a hidden compartment. In here was a small blue book. He opened it, curious to find the answers. On every page, the very same message was written.

REMEMBER ALL. REMEMEBER ALWAYS THAT CATS ONLY HAVE NINE LIVES, USE THEM WELL, USE THEM WISELY. BE GOOD.

Despite his earlier doubts, Jamie thought he had done exactly that with the one remaining life. His actions, his magic had made his school a better place. He had made his life a better life. The magic had made a difference. How GOOD was that?

He replaced the blue book in the secret compartment, returned the wooden bottom to its rightful place and carefully stacked the eight diaries plus his own into the box and shut the lid firmly. Little did he know, as he turned to walk away, new magic was stirring in the box. Amongst the diaries a yellow object appeared, waiting for the next curious Tyler.

Chapter Twenty- Two
Jamie and Billy Once Again

Back at home and just a week before the start of term at his new school, Jamie thought of the lessons he had learned from the spell, its use and the diaries in the box. However much he tried, he just could not banish the sight of Billy's defeated face as he stood head down in front of him. It haunted him. Echoes of his old friend on their first day at school, whimpering, too afraid to go in, filled his day and his dreams. . Jamie wanted to make amends. He had sought revenge and that made him as bad as Billy, he decided. He told himself that Billy was cruel and deserved it but knew from when they were small that Billy was not really bad. Circumstances and his friendship with Mouse had pushed him to it. What should he do?

The next day he was still thinking about what to do as Mum drove him to the Sports' Centre for a week of 'Fun Games'… He had grimaced when he saw the posters advertising the event. It reminded him even more of his first day at school. The event was to be run by the PE teachers from his new school as an introduction to the department but also, he suspected to tease out the talent from the new intake. Jamie liked trying new sports. He particularly wanted to try basketball which he knew was happening today.

Waving goodbye to his mum, Jamie was surprised to see Billy ambling up to the door of the Centre. There was no Mouse today. Jamie had heard from Luke that Mouse was no longer Billy's friend. Good. Billy seemed much taller than he remembered, standing head and shoulders above the other boys waiting to go in.

"Hello Billy," he shouted as he neared where he was standing. Billy mumbled something and moved with the others into the building. Jamie was trying to be friendly but it seems Billy was not yet ready to forgive him.

Inside an extremely tall man was calling together all those who wanted to play basketball. Jamie was surprised to see Billy move forward to the front of the group of excited boys and girls. He joined them. They marched steadily into a huge, cavernous hall with a hoop mounted high on the wall at either end. Jamie stood looking at them. They WERE high!

After the tall man had introduced himself as 'Coach', they spent over an hour practising skill Passing the ball, bouncing it and aiming at the basket as well as running with and without the ball. At first Jamie just wanted to put the ball to the floor and kick it. He just could not grasp the idea of bouncing it. The more he tried the more frustrated he became. The ball was heavy and hurt his wrists and it bounced anywhere except where he wanted it to go. And as for getting it through the hoop. No chance! This was a new experience for Jamie. He was good at everything he tried…

Meanwhile, Billy was performing like a 'natural'. He bounced with ease, passed and received the ball accurately and shot through the hoop every time. Jamie was too cross to notice. So the skills practice progressed, Jamie working with encouragement from 'Coach whilst Billy basked in his praise. Jamie could hear Billy's whoops of excitement which made him even more cross.

"Lets have a mini game to finish off," 'Coach' suggested with enthusiasm. Shouts of delight rang out. Jamie blew out a small puff of breath and resigned himself to humiliation.

They divided into two teams plus two subs. Jamie's game was as he expected. Sheer humiliation. He fell, he forgot to run with the ball and missed the hoop when a teammate passed the ball for him to score, Disaster. Great shouts of disappointment rang out around the hall as his teammates walked away. The next minute Jamie was taken off and replaced by one of the subs. Thank goodness. He sat on the bench, thankful to be just watching. Basketball definitely wasn't the game for him. He shrugged away that thought. You can't be good at everything. He smiled.

As he watched the game continue without him, Jamie was astounded by how well Billy played. His tall body dodging and swerving around the opposition, as he expertly bounced and passed the ball, then scoring with a perfect shot through the hoop – not once but many times. When Coach' blew time, Billy was roughly hoisted into the air by his teammates to loud cheers and whoops of delight. As the new superstar left the hall, he seemed to have grown even taller. It seemed that Billy had found HIS game. Well done Bill…

For the rest of the week, Jamie avoided the basketball hall and joined in with the football which he loved. News of Billys prowess as a basketball player filtered through the Sports Centre and there were rumours that he had already been picked for his new school's team.

"Good for him." Jamie told Luke and he real meant it. He was pleased that Billy had found something for which he could shine.

Today was the first day at his new school, the Big School' as Mum would insist on calling it. He stood at the gates watching the older boys and girls walking in confidently, laughing and joking, telling stories of their summer break. Outside the gates waited the younger children , the new starters, who were not as enthusiastic. Amongst them far above the crowd, stood Billy, trepidation plastered across his face,

Jamie was the first to venture a few steps towards a tall woman, smiling a welcome to all her new recruits. Billy hesitated, turning his head away from the kindly woman, head dropping as he turned to walk away.

"Come on everyone. Don't be shy.

This made Billy wince and move to retreat even further. On hearing those sounds, Jamie turned back and marched confidently towards Billy.

"Come on Bill. It'll be ok. Don't forget you're the new basketball star. They'll be waiting to put you through your paces and set you up for your first game. He put an arm around Billys shoulder and gently led him towards the building. Friends again.

As they entered the building, Jamie thought he heard his grandfather's voice echoing through time.

"Nice one, Jamie." It whispered, Then eight other voices joined in.

"Nice one, Jamie Tyler. The spell worked..."

Printed in Great Britain
by Amazon